AUSTRALIA

R.L. Van

Big Buddy Books
An Imprint of Abdo Publishing
abdobooks.com

abdobooks.com

Published by Abdo Publishing, a division of ABDO, PO Box 398166, Minneapolis, Minnesota 55439. Copyright © 2023 by Abdo Consulting Group, Inc. International copyrights reserved in all countries. No part of this book may be reproduced in any form without written permission from the publisher. Big Buddy Books™ is a trademark and logo of Abdo Publishing.

Printed in the United States of America, North Mankato, Minnesota
102022
012023

Design: Emily O'Malley, Mighty Media, Inc.
Production: Mighty Media, Inc.
Editor: Jessica Rusick
Cover Photograph: Aleksandar Todorovic/Shutterstock Images
Interior Photographs: Aleksandar Todorovic/Shutterstock Images, p. 6 (middle); Cahid Ahmed/Shutterstock Images, p. 13; ChameleonsEye/Shutterstock Images, pp. 9, 17, 26 (left), 27 (bottom); EcoPrint/Shutterstock Images, p. 25; Everett Collection/Shutterstock Images, p. 28; Featureflash Photo Agency/Shutterstock Images, p. 29 (top right); Gaulois_s/Shutterstock Images, p. 7 (map); hatman12/iStockphoto, pp. 27 (right), 29 (bottom); hidesy/iStockphoto, p. 27 (left); IIIShutter/iStockphoto, p. 6 (top); Julinzy/Shutterstock Images, p. 30 (flag); Justin Sullivan/Getty Images, p. 21; Logorilla/iStockphoto, p. 26 (right); Luke Shelley/Shutterstock Images, p. 15; lukulo/iStockphoto, pp. 5 (compass), 7 (compass); Mitchell Library State Library of New South Wales, p. 11; Neale Cousland/Shutterstock Images, p. 19; Pyty/Shutterstock Images, p. 5 (map); Richard Shotwell/AP Images, p. 23; SaintM Photos/iStockphoto, p. 30 (currency); Taras Vyshnya/Shutterstock Images, p. 6 (bottom); Wikimedia Commons, p. 29 (top left)
Design Elements: Mighty Media, Inc.
Country population and area figures taken from the CIA World Factbook

Library of Congress Control Number: 2022940514

Publisher's Cataloging-in-Publication Data
Names: Van, R.L., author.
Title: Australia / by R.L. Van
Description: Minneapolis, Minnesota : Abdo Publishing, 2023 | Series: Countries | Includes online resources and index.
Identifiers: ISBN 9781532199547 (lib. bdg.) | ISBN 9781098274740 (ebook)
Subjects: LCSH: Australia--Juvenile literature. | Islands of the Pacific--Juvenile literature. | Australia--History--Juvenile literature. | Geography--Juvenile literature.
Classification: DDC 994--dc23

CONTENTS

Passport to Australia 4
Important Cities 6
Australia in History 8
An Important Symbol 12
Across the Land 14
Earning a Living 16
Life in Australia 18
Famous Faces 20
A Great Country 24
Tour Book 26
Timeline 28
Australia Up Close 30
Glossary 31
Online Resources 31
Index 32

PASSPORT TO AUSTRALIA

Australia is an island between the Indian and Pacific Oceans. It is the only country that is also a **continent**. It has six states and two **territories**. More than 25 million people live there.

DID YOU KNOW?

Australia is called the "Land Down Under" because it is in Earth's southern **hemisphere**.

IMPORTANT CITIES

Canberra is Australia's **capital**. In 1927, the Australian Parliament met there for the first time.

Melbourne is Australia's largest city. It is known for its businesses, culture, and art.

Sydney is Australia's second-largest city. It is a center of business. It is also a busy port.

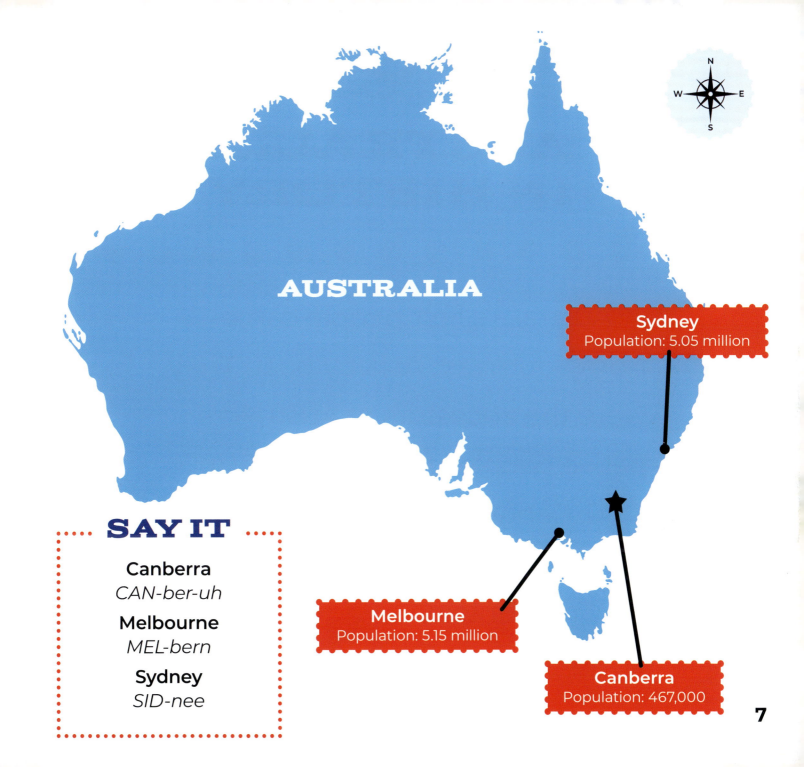

3

AUSTRALIA IN HISTORY

Australia's first people came from Southeast Asia by boat. They were the ancestors of Australia's native people, the Aborigines. In 1770, Captain James Cook claimed eastern Australia for Great Britain.

SAY IT

Aborigines
AB-uh-RIHJ-uh-neez

Aborigines created the boomerang as a tool for hunting and war.

In 1788, the British made Australia a prison colony. They sent criminals there. Over time, other British settlers arrived.

In 1901, Australia became a country. In the early 1900s, the people struggled. Over the years, the government encouraged **immigration** to Australia. This helped the country grow.

By the late 1830s, there were more free settlers than convicts in Australia.

4

AN IMPORTANT SYMBOL

Australia's flag includes a United Kingdom flag. It also has six stars. Australia is a **federal parliamentary democracy**. A prime minister leads the government. A governor-general represents the United Kingdom's king or queen. These two parts make laws together.

The flag's five smaller stars represent the Southern Cross constellation.

5

ACROSS THE LAND

Australia is mostly low and flat. The Outback covers much of it. This land has many deserts. Australia also has coasts, forests, and mountains.

Australia is home to wallabies, kangaroos, and platypuses. The country also has plants such as acacias and eucalyptus.

Many kangaroos live in the Outback.

EARNING A LIVING

Most Australians have service jobs. They work for banks, schools, restaurants, and hotels. Mining is also an important business.

Natural resources including coal, iron ore, and uranium come from Australia. Farmers produce wool, meats, grain, sugar cane, and cotton.

Wine is a major export of Australia.

LIFE IN AUSTRALIA

Most Australians live in cities. Others live in **rural** areas. Beef and other meats are popular foods. Tea, coffee, and wine are popular drinks.

Australians watch and play Australian football, rugby, soccer, and cricket. Many Australians enjoy outdoor activities and water sports.

Australian football players score points by kicking a ball through goalposts.

FAMOUS FACES

Steve Irwin was born in Essendon, Victoria. He was famous for his work with animals. In the 1990s, Irwin starred on *The Crocodile Hunter* TV show. He and his family also ran the Australia Zoo. Sadly, Irwin died in 2006. His wife and their children have continued his work.

Steve Irwin founded several charities to protect animals.

Ben Simmons is a professional basketball player in the **National Basketball Association (NBA)**. He was born in Melbourne, Victoria. Simmons has won many awards in the NBA. He is also involved in many charities, including the Ben Simmons Family Foundation.

Ben Simmons won the NBA's Rookie of the Year award in 2018.

A GREAT COUNTRY

Australia is a beautiful land with unique plants and animals. Its people and places help make the world a more interesting place.

DID YOU KNOW?
Mount Kosciuszko is Australia's highest peak, at 7,310 feet (2,228 m).

SAY IT
Kosciuszko
kah-zee-UHS-koh

Kakadu National Park is in northern Australia. Aboriginal peoples have lived there for 65,000 years.

TOUR BOOK

If you ever visit Australia, here are some places to go and things to do!

SWIM

Go snorkeling and see the beautiful colors of the Great Barrier **Reef**.

SEE

Spot dozens of Australian critters at the Australia Zoo in Beerwah, Queensland.

PLAY

Build a sandcastle on a beach in Gold Coast, Queensland.

SING

Visit the famous Sydney Opera House for a kids' tour and show.

EXPLORE

Visit the historic Old Melbourne Gaol prison museum.

TIMELINE

1895
Poet Banjo Paterson wrote the words to "Waltzing Matilda," which is considered Australia's most famous song.

1770
Captain James Cook claimed eastern Australia for Great Britain.

1906
The Australian movie *The Story of the Kelly Gang* premiered. It is thought to be the world's first full-length film.

1956

Melbourne hosted the Summer Olympic Games.

2010

Julia Gillard became Australia's first female prime minister.

1973

The Sydney Opera House opened in Sydney, New South Wales.

2017

AFL Women's, the first semiprofessional women's Australian football league, had its first season.

AUSTRALIA
UP CLOSE

Official Name
Commonwealth of Australia

Flag

Population
26,141,369 (2022 est.)
54th-most-populated country

Total Area
2,988,902 square miles
(7,741,220 sq km)
6th-largest country

National Language
English

Capital
Canberra

Currency
Australian dollar

National Anthem
"Advance Australia Fair"

Form of Government
Federal parliamentary democracy under a constitutional monarchy

GLOSSARY

capital—a city where government leaders meet.

continent—one of Earth's seven main land areas.

federal parliamentary democracy—a government in which people elect representatives to parliament, and these representatives choose a leader. The central government and the individual states and territories share power.

hemisphere (HEH-muhs-feer)—one half of Earth.

immigration—the act of leaving one's home and settling in a new country.

National Basketball Association (NBA)—a North American professional basketball league.

natural resources—useful and valuable supplies from nature.

reef—a line of underwater rocks, sand, or coral near the surface of the ocean.

rural—of or relating to open land away from towns and cities.

territory—an area that is not a state but is under the authority of a country's government.

ONLINE RESOURCES

To learn more about Australia, please visit **abdobooklinks.com** or scan this QR code. These links are routinely monitored and updated to provide the most current information available.

INDEX

Aborigines, 8, 9, 25
animals, 14, 15, 20, 21, 24, 26
Asia, 8
Australia Zoo, 20, 26

businesses, 6, 16

Canberra, 6, 7, 30
Cook, James, 8, 28

flag, 12, 13, 30
food, 16, 18

Gillard, Julia, 29
government, 6, 10, 12, 29, 30
Great Barrier Reef, 26
Great Britain, 8, 10

Indian Ocean, 4, 5
Irwin, Steve, 20, 21

Kakadu National Park, 25

language, 30

Melbourne, 6, 7, 22, 27, 29
Mount Kosciuszko, 24

natural resources, 16, 17

Outback, 14, 15

Pacific Ocean, 4, 5
Paterson, Banjo, 28
plants, 14, 16, 17, 24
population, 4, 7, 30

Simmons, Ben, 22, 23
size, 30
sports, 18, 19, 22, 23, 29
Sydney, 6, 7, 27, 29
Sydney Opera House, 27, 29

United Kingdom, 12